VIRGINIA

VIRGINIA

HELLO
U.S.A.

by Karen Sirvaitis

Lerner Publications Company

You'll find this picture of a dogwood blossom at the beginning of each chapter in this book. Dogwoods are popular in Virginia—the American dogwood tree is Virginia's state tree and its flower is the state flower. Virginians have loved dogwoods since colonial times, when Thomas Jefferson grew them at Monticello. Virginians celebrate Dogwood Day every April.

Cover (left): Shenandoah National Park in autumn. Cover (right): Monticello, Thomas Jefferson's home, near Charlottesville, Virginia. Pages 2–3: Horses and ponies swim from Assateague Island to Chincoteague Island during the annual Pony Penning. Page 3: Log cabin in the Blue Ridge Mountains.

This book is available in two editions:
Library binding by Lerner Publications Company, a division of Lerner Publishing Group
Soft cover by First Avenue Editions, an imprint of Lerner Publishing Group
241 First Avenue North
Minneapolis, MN 55401 U.S.A.

Website address: www.lernerbooks.com

Library of Congress Cataloging-in-Publication Data

Sirvaitis, Karen, 1961–
    Virginia / by Karen Sirvaitis. (Rev. and expanded 2nd ed.)
       p.   cm. — (Hello U.S.A.)
    Includes index.
    Summary: An introduction to the land, history, people, economy, and environment of Virginia.
       ISBN: 0–8225–4084–3 (lib. bdg. : alk. paper)
       ISBN: 0–8225–0797–8 (pbk. : alk. paper)
       1. Virginia—Juvenile literature. [1. Virginia.] I. Title. II. Series.
    F226.3 .S57 2002
    975.5—dc21   2001006135

Manufactured in the United States of America
1 2 3 4 5 6 – JR – 07 06 05 04 03 02

CONTENTS

Virginia's landscape is marked by mountains and fertile farmland.

THE LAND

Marshes to Mountains

irginia once stretched from the coast of the Atlantic Ocean far into the midwestern United States. Because nine states were eventually formed from its original boundaries, Virginia has been called the Mother of States.

Virginia rests midway along the East Coast. The state's present-day boundaries meet the District of Columbia and five southern states—Maryland, West Virginia, Kentucky, Tennessee, and North Carolina. Chesapeake Bay and the Atlantic Ocean wash against Virginia's coastline.

Berries from a
Jack-in-the-pulpit

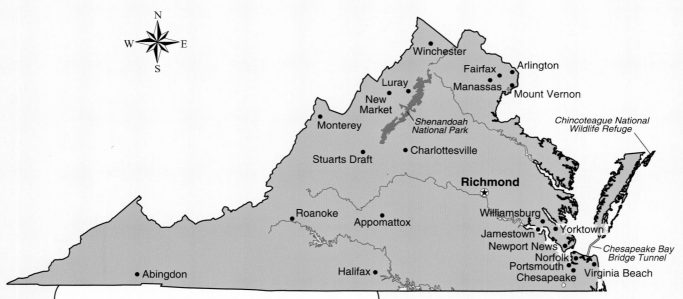

Winchester

Luray

New
Market

Monterey

Shenandoah
National Park

Fairfax
Manassas

Arlington

Mount Vernon

Chincoteague National
Wildlife Refuge

Stuarts Draft

Charlottesville

Richmond

Roanoke

Appomattox

Williamsburg

Jamestown
Newport News

Yorktown

Chesapeake Bay
Bridge Tunnel

Norfolk
Portsmouth
Chesapeake

Virginia Beach

Abingdon

Halifax

The drawing of Virginia on this page is called a political map. It shows features created by people, including cities, railways, and parks. The map on the facing page is called a physical map. It shows physical features of Virginia, such as coasts, islands, mountains, rivers, and lakes. The colors represent a range of elevations, or heights above sea level (see legend box). This map also shows the geographical regions of Virginia.

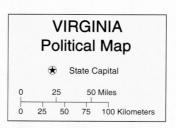

VIRGINIA
Political Map

⭐ State Capital

0	25		50 Miles
0	25	50	75	100 Kilometers

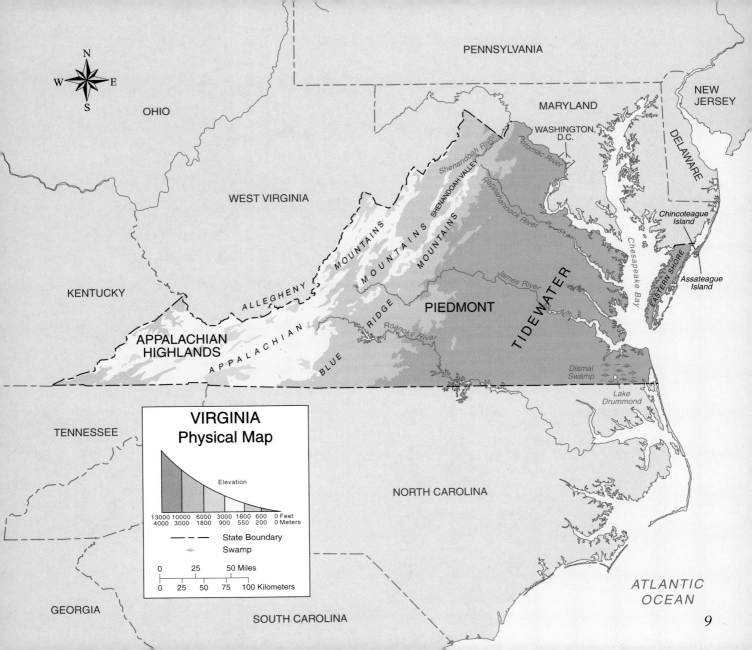

OHIO

PENNSYLVANIA

MARYLAND

NEW JERSEY

WASHINGTON, D.C.

DELAWARE

WEST VIRGINIA

Shenandoah River

Potomac River

KENTUCKY

ALLEGHENY MOUNTAINS

Rappahannock River

Chincoteague Island

APPALACHIAN HIGHLANDS

MOUNTAINS

SHENANDOAH VALLEY

MOUNTAINS

Chesapeake Bay

EASTERN SHORE

Assateague Island

APPALACHIAN

BLUE RIDGE

PIEDMONT

James River

TIDEWATER

Roanoke River

Dismal Swamp

Lake Drummond

TENNESSEE

VIRGINIA
Physical Map

Elevation

| 13000 | 10000 | 6000 | 3000 | 1800 | 600 | 0 Feet |
| 4000 | 3000 | 1800 | 900 | 550 | 200 | 0 Meters |

–––– State Boundary

⚓ Swamp

NORTH CAROLINA

0   25   50 Miles

0   25   50   75   100 Kilometers

GEORGIA

SOUTH CAROLINA

ATLANTIC OCEAN

9

Virginia's landscape varies from steep mountains to shallow **marshes** (soft wetlands). The mountains tower above western Virginia in the Appalachian Highlands region. The Piedmont and the Tidewater, two other regions, occupy the rest of the state.

The Appalachian Highlands feature part of the oldest and second longest mountain chain in North America. These peaks, called the Appalachian Mountains, took their shape slowly, beginning millions of years ago.

Wetlands are common in the low-lying areas near Virginia's coast.

The Appalachians include the Allegheny Mountains, whose high peaks kept some early Virginians from traveling farther west. Another range of the Appalachians—the Blue Ridge Mountains—lies east of the Alleghenies. All of these ranges slope downward into valleys, through which many rivers and streams flow. You may have sung songs about Shenandoah, the largest river valley in Virginia.

The rich soil of the Blue Ridge Mountain valleys makes good farmland.

The Piedmont begins where the Blue Ridge Mountains end. The word *Piedmont* comes from an Italian word that means "foot of the mountain." This region, with its clusters of grazing cattle and rows of apple trees, covers central Virginia from north to south.

Fruit growers harvest bushels of apples in the fall.

Eastern Virginia is known as the Tidewater region (also called the Atlantic Coastal Plain). Rivers, bays, and **lagoons** break up the coastal land of the Tidewater and shape Virginia's ragged shoreline. Marshes are common, especially near Chesapeake Bay, and beaches stretch along the Atlantic Ocean. A few miles inland, farmers plant crops.

Virginia's Tidewater region includes a large **peninsula** (land surrounded by water on three sides) called the Eastern Shore. Chesapeake Bay separates this peninsula from the major portion of the state. Many islands lie off the Eastern Shore.

Boaters and fishers enjoy Virginia's bays and rivers.

Several rivers—including the Shenandoah, Potomac, Rappahannock, James, and Roanoke—flow through Virginia. Large ships transport cargo on a few of the deep eastern rivers.

People have created many artificial lakes by damming, or blocking, Virginia's rivers. The state has only a few natural lakes. The largest of these is Lake Drummond. Its still waters lie within a large wetland called the Dismal Swamp, in southeastern Virginia. The **swamp** is overgrown with creeping vines and sprawling bald cypress trees.

In the spring, redbud and dogwood trees bloom near the Blue Ridge Mountains.

Sweet smelling scents from flowering shrubs, such as dogwood and mountain laurel, fill Virginia's warm spring air. The state's summers are long, lasting into October. But later that month, the trees turn shades of red, yellow, and orange, marking the beginning of fall. Winters are short, especially in the east where the occasional snow melts quickly. Rainfall is heaviest along the coast.

Forests of oak, pine, hickory, and tulip trees cover more than half of Virginia. During the spring and summer, brightly colored wildflowers highlight the lush, green valleys and the mountains.

If you venture into these mountains, you might see a black bear, a bobcat, or one of Virginia's many other animals. Along the coast, the state hosts a variety of underwater wildlife. Oysters, crabs, and other shellfish abound.

Off the Eastern Shore, bands of wild ponies roam Assateague Island. According to legend, ancestors of the ponies swam to the island from a sinking Spanish ship more than 400 years ago.

The wild ponies of Assateague Island *(right)* graze on tall grasses. A monarch caterpillar *(inset)* rests on a milkweed leaf.

John White was one of the first English artists to explore Virginia. In the late 1500s, White painted pictures *(right)* of plants, animals, and people in the Virginia region. He also made maps *(opposite page)* of Virginia's coastline.

THE HISTORY

Mother of States

magine Virginia hundreds of years ago, when European explorers stumbled upon the Americas and called them the New World. At that time—in the late 1400s—three major Native American (Indian) groups made their home in the area. They were the Cherokee, the Susquehanna, and the Algonquians.

The Algonquians lived in the Tidewater region. They knew the land well and could farm, hunt, and fish with ease. The Algonquians sometimes united their villages and followed one leader, or chief. By 1580 a chief named Powhatan ruled a group that was more than 120 villages strong, with about 9,000 inhabitants.

At the same time, across the Atlantic Ocean in the British Isles, a few leaders were planning a journey. They wanted to send some people to North America to set up a British **colony.** The British leaders believed the new colony would be rich with gold.

In 1587 the first shiploads of English people reached the eastern coast of the continent. They claimed a large part of the shore and much of the area between the Atlantic Ocean and the Pacific Ocean. They named this land Virginia, after England's ruler Elizabeth I, who never married and was known as the Virgin Queen.

The very first groups of settlers who came to the British colony of Virginia either died, disappeared, or returned to Great Britain. But the colonists who came in the spring of 1607 were more successful. They were able to establish the first British settlement to survive in the New World. (Eventually, there would be 13 British colonies.)

The first colonists arrived by ship at the mouth of what would later be called the James River. They anchored in Powhatan's territory. The newcomers unloaded their ships and named their new home Jamestown, after James I, king of Great Britain. Although many were educated, most of the residents of Jamestown had never farmed the land or built a home. They knew little about living in the wilderness.

Three ships—the *Godspeed,* the *Susan Constant,* and the *Discovery*—brought British colonists to the James River on May 13, 1607.

One man, Captain John Smith, taught the colonists to plant crops, to fish, and to build a fort to protect themselves against possible dangers. He knew their survival would be difficult, so he enforced a strict law—those who did not work did not eat. Smith also made friends with Chief Powhatan and traded kettles, jewelry, and other items to the Algonquians for much-needed food.

On May 14, 1607, the day after they arrived in the New World, the settlers began building James Fort.

Chief Powhatan was known as Wahunsenacawh before he became a chief.

Chief Powhatan suspected the strangers came to do more than trade. He feared the colonists wanted to take over the land where the Algonquians lived. The two groups often fought each other.

In 1609 Captain Smith was badly burned in a gun-powder explosion, and he returned to Britain. The following winter became known as the "starving time" because the settlers did not have enough food. Suffering from disease and hunger, they ate almost anything—even rats and snakes. Nearly all the colonists died. Just as the few survivors were ready to go home, a shipload of people and food arrived from Britain.

Trade become more important for Virginia during the 1600s. Ships began arriving more regularly, including ships that carried slaves.

Fighting between the Indians and the colonists continued. Then, in 1614, Powhatan's daughter Pocahontas married a colonist named John Rolfe. After this, the two groups lived peacefully for a time.

The colonists soon needed something valuable to send to Britain in exchange for more clothing and other necessities. They had not unearthed any gold, as they had originally hoped they would. But John Rolfe had found some tobacco seeds while shipwrecked in the West Indies. He planted the seeds after he arrived in Virginia.

Pocahontas

One of the first female heroes in Virginia's history was a young Indian, a daughter of Chief Powhatan. Her name was Pocahontas, which meant "playful child" in an Algonquian language.

Pocahontas was about 12 years old when the British landed in Virginia. Shortly after the newcomers arrived, the Algonquians captured the settlers' captain, John Smith.

One day, after a big feast, Powhatan ordered his men to bind Smith's hands. A few Indians closed in on Smith with raised clubs. But before the men could strike, Pocahontas lunged between Smith and the weapons. Chief Powhatan ordered that Smith be released.

The relieved captain believed Pocahontas had saved his life. If she did prevent his death, Pocahontas also saved the colonists

who depended upon Smith for their survival. Pocahontas and Smith became good friends. Smith taught her to speak English, and she helped Smith learn Algonquian.

In 1614, several years after the Indians captured Smith, Pocahontas married colonist John Rolfe. Because of the marriage, the Indians and the settlers were friendlier toward each other.

Pocahontas died at about the age of 22. She and Rolfe were visiting Great Britain when she caught a disease called smallpox. Her husband and their young son, Thomas, remained in Britain, where the boy went to school. Thomas later returned to Virginia and raised a family. Some Virginians claim to be descendants of the heroine's family.

John Rolfe introduced tobacco to the New World. It became the colonists' first moneymaking crop.

Tobacco grew well in Virginia's soil and climate. Planters sent samples of the product to Britain. Smoking it became very popular there. Before long, the colonists were growing the plant almost everywhere—even between cracks in the streets! Rich tobacco farmers built **plantations** (large farms) on what had been the Indians' homeland.

At first, the colonists used indentured servants—people who were forced to work for other people for several years before earning their freedom—as their labor force. The first black people in Virginia were indentured servants. But within 50 years, colonists would use black people as slaves.

Meanwhile, the Indians were trying to get back their land. In 1622 they attacked the colonists, killing more than 300 people. The last attempt to get rid of the British ended in 1644. Gradually, the farmers forced the Native Americans farther and farther west.

During the 1600s and 1700s, both the British and the French explored parts of North America and claimed some of the same land. In 1754 the two groups began fighting the French and Indian War to settle these claims. Many Indians sided with the French, but the French lost the war in 1763. Soldiers from Virginia fought bravely for the British. One of these soldiers was George Washington.

To help pay the costs of the French and Indian War, Britain taxed the colonists on everyday items such as sugar and tea. This upset the colonists.

Nathaniel Bacon *(above, right)* led colonists who wanted fewer trade laws and better protection from Indians in a rebellion against Virginia's governor, William Berkeley *(above, left)*. The rebels burned down the Governor's Palace in Jamestown in 1676.

A small group of Virginians gathered to talk about the new British laws. Members of the group included Patrick Henry, Thomas Jefferson, and George Washington.

In 1774 a few of these people met with leaders from the other colonies at the First Continental Congress in Philadelphia. The Congress decided that unless Britain stopped charging unreasonable

Patrick Henry urged his fellow Virginians to gather an army against Britain. His speech ended with the famous words "Give me liberty or give me death!"

Virginian Thomas Jefferson wrote the Declaration of Independence in 1776. Jefferson, who became the third president of the United States, died on July 4, 1826, exactly 50 years after the signing of the declaration.

taxes, the colonists would not buy British goods.

Britain, however, kept taxing tea. Tension mounted, and the first gunshot of the American Revolution (the war between Britain and the 13 colonies) was fired in Massachusetts in 1775. George Washington was made commander in chief of the colonial forces.

On May 15, 1776, Virginians declared their colony independent of British rule. Soon afterward, on July 4, 1776, the Continental Congress approved Thomas Jefferson's Declaration of Independence, which stated that all 13 colonies were breaking ties with Britain.

Most of the fighting in the revolution took place in other colonies, but the last major battle ended at Yorktown, Virginia, in 1781. By this time, the Americans had formed an alliance with France, which was still an enemy of Britain. With the help of the French army and navy, colonial forces led by George Washington defeated British troops. The war officially ended in 1783, when both sides signed a peace agreement.

George Washington's first portrait was painted when he was already 40 years old.

At Yorktown, Virginia, in 1781, British troops surrendered to colonial forces.

George Washington worked with members of the Continental Congress to write a **constitution.** After the people of a colony accepted the laws in the constitution, that colony became a member of the Union—that is, the United States of America.

Virginia became the 10th state on June 25, 1788. One year later, George Washington became the first president of the United States.

As the young nation grew during the 1800s, it experienced many changes. For example, the Northern states built many factories, while the Southern states continued to farm. The lifestyles of Northerners and Southerners became very different. They disagreed on many issues, including the South's wide use of slaves.

By 1861 several Southern states had withdrawn from the Union to form the Confederate States of America, a separate country that allowed slavery. Abraham Lincoln, who was then the U.S. president, sent troops into the South. The Civil War (1861–1865) between the Northern and Southern states had begun.

Virginians did not want to go to war. They had waited until the North declared war before joining the Confederate, or Southern, army. That same year, Richmond, Virginia, became the capital of the Confederate States.

Slaves typically worked long, hard days on their master's plantation.

Robert E. Lee disliked slavery, but he remained loyal to his home state during the Civil War.

Most Virginians who lived in the state's northwestern mountains still supported the North. In 1863 this part of Virginia became a separate state called West Virginia.

Robert E. Lee, a Virginian, led the Confederates to many victories during the Civil War. But in 1865, General Lee and his troops were forced to surrender at Appomattox, Virginia. President Lincoln had already called for all the slaves in the Confederate States to be freed.

The war was over, but for Virginians more hardship lay ahead. More Civil War battles had been fought in Virginia than in any other state. Cities and plantations lay in ruins.

Before Confederate soldiers surrendered Richmond to the Union army, they set the city on fire.

During the period known as **Reconstruction,** the U.S. government helped reconstruct, or rebuild, the war-torn South. Slowly, Virginia recovered. Virginians approved a new state constitution and in 1870 rejoined the United States.

Virginia's people began to rely not only on farming but also on manufacturing and mining, especially of coal. Factories were built, and their owners hired workers to make cloth, cigarettes, and ships. These new jobs encouraged people to stay in the state.

In 1912 a Virginian, Woodrow Wilson, was elected president. During Wilson's term, World War I (1914–1918) broke out in Europe. The U.S. military trained soldiers and pilots at camps set up in Virginia. During the war, the U.S. government built the Norfolk Naval Base, which became the largest naval base in the country. In the early 1940s, Virginia again became a military base for U.S. soldiers serving in World War II (1939–1945).

After the war, black people united to demand their **civil rights,** or personal freedoms. Black people had been segregated (separated or kept apart) from

white people. Blacks and whites were not allowed, for example, to attend the same schools. And schools for black students were generally inferior to those for white students. In 1954, however, the U.S. Supreme Court ruled that students of all colors must share classrooms.

Before the U.S. Supreme Court made segregation illegal, black people had to use separate entrances to public buildings.

Several of Virginia's schools closed because some people still wanted to keep students segregated. In 1959 the U.S. Supreme Court ordered the state to follow the law, and all but one school system reopened that year.

Two third graders greet each other on the first day their school is open to both black and white students. This Virginia school wasn't desegregated until 1964.

These political issues didn't keep the state economy from booming, however. In the late 1950s and throughout the 1960s, Virginia's industries flourished. The state continued to attract new business, and the manufacture of textiles (cloth), chemicals, electrical equipment, and transportation equipment became big business.

During the mid-1900s, many Virginians had jobs in factories like this textile mill.

During this economic boom, the state grew in other ways. In the past, Virginians had to drive through neighboring Maryland or take a ferryboat across the bay to reach the Eastern Shore. But in 1964, the state completed the Chesapeake Bay Bridge Tunnel. Together, the bridge and tunnel are 18 miles long. They make it possible to drive across the bay between Norfolk and the peninsula.

During the 1970s and 1980s, concern over air pollution caused the nation to search for cleaner and cheaper sources of energy. As a result, Virginia's coal-mining companies started losing money.

Virginia's tobacco industry declined in the 1990s. In 1998, 46 states reached an agreement with the five largest tobacco manufacturers. The agreement limits how tobacco companies can advertise their products. The manufacturers must also pay money to tobacco-producing states such as Virginia to stop them from relying only on the crop.

On September 11, 2001, terrorists hijacked a passenger plane and crashed it into the Pentagon, the U.S. defense headquarters, in Arlington, Virginia. A

section of the large, five-sided office building was destroyed. Nearly 200 people—many of them Virginians—were killed. The same day, two hijacked planes crashed into the World Trade Center in New York City, causing the collapse of the twin towers and killing thousands of people. Another hijacked plane crashed in the Pennsylvania countryside. The strikes were the worst terrorist attacks in U.S. history.

The terrorist attacks had hit the center of American military power—the Pentagon. But Americans stood united as they faced their loss. Virginians look to the future with determination and resolve to carry on their rich traditons.

Days after the September 11 tragedy, cleanup efforts began at the Pentagon.

Virginia shipbuilders make both military and commercial vessels. This aircraft carrier was built by the Newport News Shipbuilding Company in Newport News, Virginia.

PEOPLE & ECONOMY

Rich Traditions

Virginia is a land of tradition and innovation, where the past meets the present. More than 7 million people live in the state. As in the 1600s, some people farm tobacco fields or fish Chesapeake Bay. Others, however, work in computerized textile mills or with high-tech military equipment.

About one-fourth of Virginia's people live in rural areas, and many of them are farmers. Most Virginians live and work in or near the cities of Norfolk, Arlington, Virginia Beach, Roanoke, and Richmond—the capital.

The cities in northeastern Virginia are home to thousands of people who commute to work in neighboring Washington, D.C. The huge office building known as the Pentagon stands in Arlington, a city near the nation's capital. About 24,000 people work in the Pentagon for the U.S. Department of Defense. Farther south, in Norfolk, the U.S. government operates the Norfolk Naval Base.

Sailors serve their country on ships like these docked at Norfolk Naval Base.

About 70 percent of Virginia's population are white people whose ancestors came from Great Britain or Germany. African Americans make up about 19 percent of the population. Native Americans number less than 1 percent of Virginia's population. Most of Virginia's recent **immigrants** (newcomers) are Latino or Southeast Asian.

Virginians built the country's first free, or public, school in 1634. They called it Syms Free School. Many children could not attend Syms, however, because they lived too far away. Most Virginians could get an education after the Civil War, when the state started paying for public education. In modern-day Virginia, more than 1 million children attend the state's public schools.

Southeast Asians are among Virginia's fastest-growing immigrant groups.

During the summer, Virginians sunbathe and water-ski at Chesapeake Bay and the Atlantic Ocean. Sailboats, motorboats, and yachts crowd the waters and dock along the shores of the bay. People also hike on the trails in the Appalachians—a place to get plenty of exercise while admiring the scenery.

Outdoor activities, including hiking and boating, are popular in Virginia.

Fox hunting, a tradition the colonists carried over from Britain, is still a familiar sport in northern Virginia. Groups of riders on horseback, surrounded by dozens of hunting dogs, often spend hours tracking foxes on the grounds of old plantations.

Brightly dressed fox hunters and their dogs head for the woods.

Colonial history comes to life with demonstrations of the Fife and Drum Corps of Williamsburg. Fife players and drummers once accompanied military units.

The people who live in Virginia's Appalachian Highlands follow customs that have been passed down from generation to generation. Fiddlers play lively, toe-tapping music at local square dances. Some craftspeople make musical instruments called dulcimers. These stringed instruments and other artworks are displayed each August at the Highlands Festival in Abingdon.

Virginians are proud of their rich past. Part of Williamsburg, the state's capital from 1699 to 1780, has been rebuilt to look the way it did in colonial days. Workers dress in period costumes—women wear bonnets and long, full skirts, and men dress in ruffled shirts, knee breeches, and powdered wigs.

The Museum of the Confederacy in Richmond displays uniforms, weapons, and documents from the Civil War. The Mariners' Museum in Newport News features the history of ships and shipping in the United States. And the Barter Theatre, situated in the mountains, presents many well-known plays. It got its name when it opened in 1933, during an economic crisis called the Great Depression. Unable to pay for tickets, people bartered—or traded—pigs, chickens, flowers, and other goods for admission.

Confederate president Jefferson Davis lived in this Virginia mansion during the Civil War. Known as the White House of the Confederacy, the building is part of the Museum of the Confederacy in Richmond.

Cows graze in a Virginia pasture.

Virginia farmers raise hogs as livestock.

Tobacco, the crop that grew well for Virginia's colonists, is still one of Virginia's leading crops. Only a small number of farmers actually grow the plant, but tobacco processing employs many other Virginians. Most of Virginia's farmers sell milk, beef, chickens, turkeys, and hogs. Virginia is famous for its Smithfield hams, which come from hogs that were fed mostly peanuts.

Virginia's most important mineral is coal, which is dug from deep underground. When burned, coal releases energy. Many power plants across the United States use this form of energy to produce electricity. Virginia is a leading coal-producing state.

Many Virginians work in factories that make chemicals, ships, clothing, or electrical equipment. Some people fish for a living. They bring in oysters, crabs, clams, and scallops from Chesapeake Bay. At nearby factories, these shellfish are packaged to be sold.

Coal is the leading mined product of Virginia. It is transported from the Appalachian Highlands in railroad cars.

VIRGINIA
Economic Map

The symbols on this map show where different economic activities take place in Virginia. The legend below explains what each symbol stands for.

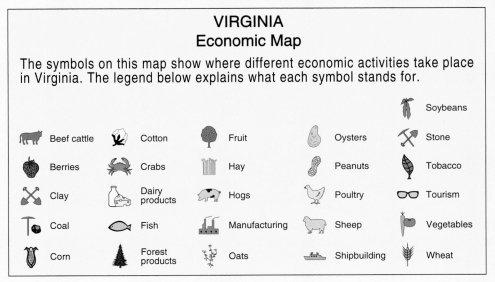

				Soybeans
Beef cattle	Cotton	Fruit	Oysters	Stone
Berries	Crabs	Hay	Peanuts	Tobacco
Clay	Dairy products	Hogs	Poultry	Tourism
Coal	Fish	Manufacturing	Sheep	Vegetables
Corn	Forest products	Oats	Shipbuilding	Wheat

A worker examines the propeller of a commercial ship that needs repair.

Virginia's products are shipped from several major port cities in the state. Large freighters anchor easily in the deep harbors of Chesapeake Bay. The harbors in the Norfolk area are some of the leading ports in the United States.

Most Virginians have jobs that provide services to people and businesses. These service workers include doctors, lawyers, and bankers. Other service workers sell cars or houses. They are employed in department stores, in supermarkets, and at telephone companies.

Because Virginia is so close to Washington, D.C., many people work for the federal government. Some of these Virginians work for the Department of Defense and the Central Intelligence Agency or on military bases. Employees of the state government include teachers, park rangers, and city and state officials.

Virginia continues to be an economic leader, drawing new industry and businesses to the state in large numbers. By 1998 the state had the world's largest concentration of information technology, telecommunications, and Internet companies. As the birthplace of the Internet, which was developed by the Pentagon, Virginia is well on its way to becoming a world center for information technology and telecommunications.

Boats crowd Chesapeake Bay during summer months.

THE ENVIRONMENT

A Changing Ecosystem

 hesapeake Bay is the nation's largest estuary, a place where ocean saltwater meets freshwater from rivers. On the bay, Virginians harvest oysters and load them onto sailing vessels called skipjacks. But the skipjacks are not as full of shellfish as they were 20 years ago. Boaters still cruise the bay in colorful sailboats, but some swimmers have chosen to go elsewhere. Life in and around the bay is changing because parts of the bay's ecosystem are changing.

Chesapeake Bay's ecosystem includes more than just marine life. Birds such as bald eagles are also part of it.

An ecosystem is a community of living and nonliving things in nature, including plants, animals, soil, air, and water. Each living member in an ecosystem needs nutrients (nourishment needed for health) and depends on the other members in its ecosystem for these nutrients.

Nutrients occur naturally in the bay's water. But they also enter the water from sources outside the bay. For example, to make crops and lawns grow better, people apply fertilizers. Fertilizers contain nutrients in the form of nitro-

Fertilizers used in Virginia's fields drain into the bay.

gen and phosphorus. Eventually, rainwater washes some of the fertilizer into the bay or into rivers that drain into the bay. This process is called **nutrient runoff.**

Another source that brings nutrients into the Chesapeake Bay is wastewater. Wastewater is the water that carries sewage from homes, businesses, and industries to sewage treatment plants. Wastewater contains many nutrients that come from the sewage it carries. When wastewater reaches the treatment plants, it is filtered, cleansed, and then released into rivers or the bay. Treating wastewater, however, does not remove any of its nutrients.

Forty-eight rivers, some with tributaries (arms) as far north as New York, flow into Chesapeake Bay. These waterways carry both nutrient runoff and treated wastewater from six states and more than 15 million people. The great number of nutrients entering the bay has changed its ecosystem. Some of its members are multiplying rapidly, while others are dying.

Pollution in the bay comes from factories, as well as from homes and businesses.

For instance, algae—small rootless plants that live just under the water's surface—feed on the many nutrients in the bay and grow very thick. A certain amount of algae is good. They are a source of food for fish. But the algae in the bay are so thick that the fish do not eat all of them. Eventually, the plants that do not get eaten die and sink to the bottom of the bay.

Algae grow in a river that flows into Chesapeake Bay.

Dead plants are food for bacteria (tiny, one-celled organisms). The bacteria at the bottom of the bay multiply easily because of all the dead plants there. All these bacteria use a lot of oxygen, another substance needed by living things.

The bottom of the Chesapeake does not have enough oxygen for both the bacteria and all the bay's underwater wildlife. When bacteria thrive, many of the fish and oysters, which cannot get enough oxygen, either die or leave the area.

Washington, D.C., and the states of Virginia, Maryland, and Pennsylvania are working together to watch the bay's health carefully. By reducing pollution and by teaching farmers and homeowners to use less fertilizer on their crops and lawns, they hope to improve the bay's health.

And in 2000, the Chesapeake Bay Program adopted a new agreement known as Chesapeake 2000. This agreement will guide the restoration efforts until the year 2010. With everyone's participation, Chesapeake Bay may have a better future.

Fun Facts

You can thank a Virginian, Thomas Jefferson, for the tomatoes in your salad. Before he bit into one in the late 1700s, many Americans believed the fruit to be poisonous.

Virginians who want to help keep their state clean can "Adopt-a-Spot." Adopted spots include public lands and sections of roads or streets up to two miles. Armed with brooms and trash bags, volunteers are in charge of keeping their adopted spot free of litter.

In Arlington, Virginia, more than 15,000 meals are served each day at the Pentagon, one of the largest office buildings in the world.

Virginia's Blue Ridge Mountains got their name from their trees. From a distance, the trees appear to be blue.

What do Presidents George Washington, Thomas Jefferson, James Madison, James Monroe, William Henry Harrison, John Tyler, Zachary Taylor, and Woodrow Wilson have in common? They were all born in Virginia. More U.S. presidents were born in Virginia than in any other state, giving it the nickname "Mother of Presidents."

The wives of six presidents were born in Virginia. Martha Washington, Martha Jefferson, Rachel Jackson, Letitia Tyler, Ellen Arthur, and Edith Wilson all came from Virginia.

A hiker surveys the Blue Ridge Mountain landscape.

STATE SONG

"Carry Me Back to Old Virginia" was written in 1875 by James A. Bland, a well-known black songwriter of the time. It was officially adopted as Virginia's state song in 1940. Many people have objected to the song's lyrics, which refer to slavery. In 1997 the song was declared "state song emeritus," or former state song. The state plans to replace it with a new state song.

CARRY ME BACK TO OLD VIRGINIA

Words and music by James A. Bland

Car - ry me back to old Vir - gin - ia, That's where the cot - ton and the

corn and ta - ters grow, There's where the birds war - ble sweet in the spring - time,

There's where this old wand' - rer's heart does long to go. There's where I la - bored so

hard for old Mas - sa, Day af - ter day in the field of yel - low corn,

No place on earth do I love more sin - cere - ly Than old Vir - gin - ia, the state where I was born.

A VIRGINIA RECIPE

Virginia's Shenandoah Valley is home to large apple orchards. You can add apples to peanut butter, another of the state's chief food products, for a tasty treat.

PEANUT BUTTER AND APPLE COOKIES

½ cup butter
½ cup creamy peanut butter
½ cup sugar
½ cup light brown sugar
1 egg
½ teaspoon vanilla

1 large apple
2 cups flour
¾ teaspoon baking soda
¼ teaspoon salt
¼ teaspoon cinnamon
½ cup additional sugar

1. Ask an adult to preheat oven to 350°F.
2. Have an adult help peel apple and remove core. Then finely grate or chop apple.
3. Mix butter and peanut butter. Add sugars, egg, vanilla, and apple, in that order.
4. Mix flour, baking soda, salt, and cinnamon. Stir into creamed mixture.
5. With teaspoon, roll mixture into ½-inch balls. Roll each ball in extra sugar.
6. Place balls on ungreased cookie sheet, 1 inch apart. Flatten slightly by pressing each ball with back of fork.
7. With an adult's help, bake for 10 to 12 minutes, until cookies are lightly browned. Remove from pan to finish cooling. Store in an airtight container.

Makes 4 dozen cookies.

HISTORICAL TIMELINE

1580 Chief Powhatan rules a strong Algonquian nation in the Virginia area.

1587 English settlers arrive in what later becomes Virginia.

1607 Colonists build the Jamestown colony in what later becomes Virginia.

1622 Indians attack English settlers, killing more than 300 colonists.

1754 Fighting breaks out between British colonists and the French, starting the French and Indian War (1754–1763).

1775 The American Revolution (1775–1783) begins.

1776 Thomas Jefferson writes the Declaration of Independence, in which the 13 colonies break ties with Great Britain.

1781 Lord Cornwallis, commander of the British army, surrenders at Yorktown, Virginia.

1788 Virginia becomes the 10th state to join the Union.

1789 George Washington is elected as the first president of the United States.

1861 The Civil War (1861–1865) begins. More Civil War battles are fought in Virginia than in any other state.

1863 The northwestern part of Virginia becomes West Virginia.

1865 General Robert E. Lee surrenders at Appomattox, Virginia, ending the Civil War.

1917 Construction begins on Norfolk Naval Base.

1954 The U.S. Supreme Court rules that racial segregation is against the law. Some Virginia schools close to protest the decision.

1959 The Supreme Court orders Virginia to reopen schools closed in 1954.

1964 The Chesapeake Bay Bridge Tunnel connects the Eastern Shore to mainland Virginia.

1989 Virginians elect the nation's first black governor, Douglas Wilder.

1998 Tobacco manufacturers agree to pay money to Virginia and other tobacco-producing states in order to reduce reliance on the crop.

2001 A hijacked passenger plane crashes into the Pentagon, killing nearly 200 people. The tragedy is part of a major terrorist attack on the United States.

OUTSTANDING VIRGINIANS

Arthur Ashe

Arthur Ashe (1943–1993) was a professional tennis player from Richmond. In 1975 he became the first black person to win the men's singles title in tennis at Wimbledon, England. In 1992 he revealed that he had become infected with the virus that causes AIDS through a tainted blood transfusion. Until his death in 1993, Ashe was an activist devoted to educating the public about the disease.

Pearl Bailey

Pearl Bailey (1918–1990), a singer and actress, was born in Newport News, Virginia. Bailey is best known for her starring role in the Broadway musical *Hello, Dolly!* She made many television appearances, and hosted her own show, *The Pearl Bailey Show*, in 1971.

Warren Beatty (born 1937) is an actor, director, and producer from Richmond. He starred in the films *Splendor in the Grass, Bonnie and Clyde, Heaven Can Wait,* and *Dick Tracy.* He is the brother of actress Shirley MacLaine.

Warren Beatty

Harry F. Byrd Sr. (1887–1966), a politician, helped reorganize the state government while he was governor of Virginia from 1926 to 1930. Byrd became a U.S. senator representing Virginia in 1933. He served for 30 years.

Willa Cather (1873–1947), a writer, was born in Winchester, Virginia. In 1922 Cather won a Pulitzer Prize for her novel *One of Ours.* Her most famous novels, which are noted for portrayals of frontier life on the American plains, include *My Ántonia, O Pioneers!,* and *Death Comes for the Archbishop.*

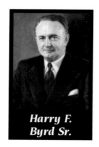

Harry F. Byrd Sr.

William Clark (1770–1838) was an explorer born in Caroline County, Virginia. From 1804 to 1806, Clark and Meriwether Lewis explored the western territories that the United States had just purchased from France. After the journey, President Thomas Jefferson made Clark brigadier general of the militia for the Louisiana (later Missouri) Territory as well as superintendent of Indian affairs.

William Clark

Patsy Cline (1932–1963) was a country-music singer born in Winchester, Virginia. Cline's career was cut short when she died in a plane crash. Her hit singles include "Walkin' After Midnight," "I Fall to Pieces," and "Crazy."

Ella Fitzgerald (1917–1996) was a jazz singer who won 12 Grammy Awards. Born in Newport News, Virginia, Fitzgerald was called the First Lady of Song. Her songs include "A-Tisket, A-Tasket" and "Love and Kisses."

Ella Fitzgerald

William Henry Harrison (1773–1841) became the ninth president of the United States in 1840. His famous campaign slogan, "Tippecanoe and Tyler Too," came from the nickname (Tippecanoe) he earned during an Indian battle and from the last name of his running mate, John Tyler. Harrison died of pneumonia after only one month in office. Harrison was born in the county of Charles City, Virginia.

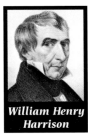

William Henry Harrison

Patrick Henry (1736–1799) was an American patriot and speaker born in Studley, Virginia. Before the American Revolution broke out, he urged colonists to break ties with Great Britain. His most famous speech includes the words "Give me liberty or give me death!" Henry served as independent Virginia's first governor, from 1776 until 1779 and from 1784 until 1786.

Patrick Henry

Robert E. Lee

Meriwether Lewis

Shirley MacLaine

Moses Malone

Thomas Jefferson (1743–1826) was an inventor and politician born in Shadwell, Virginia. Jefferson is best known as the author of the Declaration of Independence and as the third president of the United States. Jefferson said, "It is wonderful how much may be done if we are always doing." He took his own advice and spent his spare time designing buildings and inventing gadgets. He designed the University of Virginia, Virginia's state capitol building, and his home, Monticello.

Robert E. Lee (1807–1870) was a military general born in Stratford, Virginia. A gifted strategist, Lee became the commander of the Confederate army during the Civil War. Although he fought for the South, he wished to see the United States remain one country. After the war, Lee became president of Washington College (later Washington and Lee University) in Lexington, Virginia.

Meriwether Lewis (1774–1809), an explorer born near Charlottesville, Virginia, was one of the leaders of the Lewis and Clark expedition. The information he and William Clark gathered on their two-year exploration of the West encouraged pioneers to settle the new territory.

Shirley MacLaine (born 1934) is an actress, dancer, and author. She has starred in many films, including *Guarding Tess, Steel Magnolias,* and *Terms of Endearment.* The sister of actor Warren Beatty, MacLaine grew up in Richmond.

Moses Malone (born 1955) is a basketball player who grew up in Petersburg, Virginia. A center who played for several NBA teams such as the Atlanta Hawks, the Philadelphia 76ers, and the San Antonio Spurs, Malone retired in 1994 after 18 years on the court. He was inducted into the National Basketball Hall of Fame in 2001.

Cyrus Hall McCormick (1809–1884) was an inventor from Rockbridge County, Virginia. He invented a machine called a reaper. With this invention, farmers no longer had to cut grain from their fields by hand. They could harvest the grain faster than ever before.

George C. Scott (1927–1999) was an actor from Wise, Virginia. His most famous movies include *The Hanging Tree, The Hustler,* and *Patton.* Scott was nominated for Academy Awards for all three movies but refused to accept the nominations.

George C. Scott

Nat Turner (1800–1831) was born a slave in Southampton County, Virginia. In 1831 he and his followers led a rebellion against slavery, killing 60 slave owners and freeing the laborers. He planned to free more slaves but was captured and hanged.

Nat Turner

Booker T. Washington (1856–1915) was an educator and writer born in Franklin County, Virginia. In 1881 Washington founded the Tuskegee Normal and Industrial Institute (later Tuskegee University), a college in Alabama for black students. He wrote his autobiography, *Up from Slavery,* in 1901.

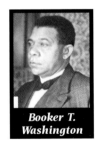

Booker T. Washington

George Washington (1732–1799) was a general and politician born in Westmoreland County, Virginia. Washington became commander in chief of the colonial armies in the American Revolution (1775–1783). He served as the first president of the United States from 1789 until 1797. Washington is often called the Father of Our Country.

L. Douglas Wilder (born 1931) was elected governor of Virginia in 1989. Born in Richmond, Wilder was the first black person ever to be elected governor in the United States.

Tom Wolfe (born 1930) is an author from Richmond. His bestsellers include *The Electric Kool-Aid Acid Test* and *The Bonfire of the Vanities.*

Tom Wolfe

FACTS-AT-A-GLANCE

Nickname: Old Dominion

Song: no official song

Motto: *Sic Semper Tyrannis* (Thus Always to Tyrants)

Flower: American dogwood

Tree: American dogwood

Bird: northern cardinal

Dog: American fox hound

Shell: oyster

Fossil: *Chesapecten jeffersonius*

Date and ranking of statehood: June 25, 1788, the 10th state

Capital: Richmond

Area: 39,598 square miles

Rank in area, nationwide: 37th

Average January temperature: 36° F

Average July temperature: 75° F

Virginia's flag has been in use since 1861. The flag features the state seal, which is based on a design made in 1776.

POPULATION GROWTH

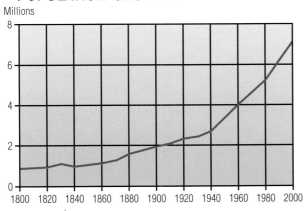

Millions

This chart shows how Virginia's population has grown from 1800 to 2000.

Virginia's state seal was designed in 1776. It shows Virtue defeating Tyranny, symbolizing the state's independence from England. On the back are the Roman goddesses of eternity, liberty, and agriculture.

Population: 7,078,515 (2000 census)

Rank in population, nationwide: 12th

Major cities and populations: (2000 census) Virginia Beach (425,257), Norfolk (234,403), Chesapeake (199,184), Richmond (197,790), Arlington (189,453)

U.S. senators: 2

U.S. representatives: 11

Electoral votes: 13

Natural resources: basalt, clay, coal, granite, gypsum, limestone, marble, natural gas, petroleum, salt, sandstone, shale, soil, zinc

Agricultural products: apples, beef cattle, chickens, corn, hay, hogs, milk, peanuts, potatoes, soybeans, tobacco, tomatoes, turkeys

Fishing industry: clams, crab, flounder, menhaden, oysters, scallops, striped bass

Manufactured goods: chemicals, electrical equipment, food products, plastic products, printed materials, rubber products, tobacco products, transportation equipment

WHERE VIRGINIANS WORK

Services—62 percent (services includes jobs in trade; community, social and personal services; finance, insurance, and real estate; transportation, communication, and utilities)

Government—19 percent

Manufacturing—10 percent

Construction—6 percent

Agriculture—3 percent

Mining—less than 1 percent

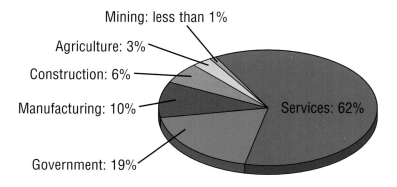

Mining: less than 1%
Agriculture: 3%
Construction: 6%
Manufacturing: 10%
Government: 19%
Services: 62%

GROSS STATE PRODUCT

Services—61 percent

Government—18 percent

Manufacturing—15 percent

Construction—5 percent

Agriculture—1 percent

Mining—less than 1 percent

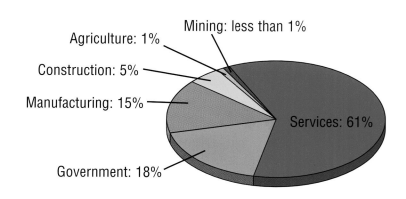

Agriculture: 1%
Mining: less than 1%
Construction: 5%
Manufacturing: 15%
Services: 61%
Government: 18%

VIRGINIA WILDLIFE

Mammals: black bear, bobcat, deer, elk, fox, muskrat, opossum, rabbits, raccoon, white-tailed deer

Birds: American bittern, bald eagle, brown pelican, ducks, geese, quail, ruffed grouse, snowy egret, turkey vulture

Amphibians and reptiles: American toad, bog turtle, corn snake, green treefrog, ground skink, leatherback sea turtle, northern copperhead

Fish: alewife, bass, carp, clam, crab, drum, flounder, mackerel, menhaden, oyster, perch, pickerel, pike, trout

Trees: ash, beech, birch, black tupelo, hemlock, hickory, locust, maple, red cedar, spruce, sweet gum, tulip tree

Wild plants: azalea, blue lobelia, flowering dogwood, morning glory, mountain laurel, piratebush, redbud, rhododendron, violet

Snowy egret

PLACES TO VISIT

Arlington National Cemetery, Arlington

This 612-acre cemetery is a shrine to thousands of American veterans. Visitors can see various memorials, including the Tomb of the Unknowns, the gravesite of John F. Kennedy, and the Space Shuttle *Challenger* Memorial.

Bayly Art Museum, Charlottesville

The Bayly Art Museum at the University of Virginia displays ancient art, Native American textiles, American paintings and sculpture, modern art, and more.

Caledon Natural Area, King George County

Caledon is the summer home to one of the largest gatherings of American bald eagles. Limited tours of the area are available, and a visitor center offers exhibits.

Children's Museum of Virginia, Portsmouth

Visitors to the largest children's museum in Virginia learn about science and history through interactive exhibits and a planetarium. The museum also features an antique toy and model train collection.

Colonial National Historical Park, Yorktown

The park features sites that represent the beginning and the end of English colonial America. The park includes Jamestown, the first permanent English settlement in North America, and Yorktown Battlefield, the site of final major battle of the American Revolutionary War.

Colonial Williamsburg, Williamsburg

The nation's largest outdoor history museum, Colonial Williamsburg consists of 173 acres, 88 original buildings, and hundreds of homes, shops, and public buildings. Several indoor museums also teach visitors about life in Virginia in the 1700s.

Luray Caverns, Luray

Luray Caverns are the largest caverns on the East Coast. Some of the enormous caverns are filled with stone columns. Visitors can explore the nearby Car and Carriage Caravan Museum, which exhibits cars, carriages, and coaches dating back to 1725.

Manassas National Battlefield Park, Manassas

Site of the first major battle of the Civil War, the park offers battle maps, an exhibit of equipment, battle memorabilia, presentations, and a tour of the battlefield.

Monticello, Charlottesville

Explore Thomas Jefferson's famous home, including the botanical gardens and the 5,000-acre plantation.

Mount Vernon Estate and Gardens, Mount Vernon

Mount Vernon served as George Washington's home from 1759 until his death in 1799. Visitors to the estate can tour the mansion, gardens, museum exhibitions, and Washington's tomb.

Virginia Marine Science Museum, Virginia Beach

Visitors can learn about the waters of Virginia at this museum, which is home to more than 800,000 gallons of aquariums. The museum features interactive exhibits and boat trips for dolphin watching, whale watching, and ocean collections.

ANNUAL EVENTS

African American History Month at Monticello, Charlottesville—*February*

Highland Maple Festival, Monterey—*March*

Dogwood Festival, Charlottesville—*April*

Shenandoah Apple Blossom Festival, Winchester—*May*

The Battle of New Market Reenactment, New Market—*May*

Bluemont Concert Series, central and northern Virginia—*June–August*

Sun and Sand Beach Weekend, Stuarts Draft—*June*

Pony Penning and Auction, Chincoteague—*July*

Virginia Cantaloupe Festival, Halifax—*July*

Neptune Festival, Virginia Beach—*September*

Virginia State Fair, Richmond—*September–October*

Festival of Lights and Carols, Fairfax—*December*

LEARN MORE ABOUT VIRGINIA

BOOKS

General

Barrett, Tracy. *Virginia.* New York: Benchmark Books, 1997. For older readers.

Blashfield, Jean F. *Virginia.* New York: Children's Press, 1999. For older readers.

Cocke, William. *A Historical Album of Virginia.* Brookfield, CT: Millbrook Press, 1995.

Special Interest

Ferris, Jeri Chase. *Thomas Jefferson: Father of Liberty.* Minneapolis: Carolrhoda Books, Inc., 1998. This biography covers the highlights of Jefferson's life, including his childhood in Virginia, the construction of Monticello, and his political career. For older readers.

Holler, Anne. *Pocahontas: Powhatan Peacemaker.* New York: Chelsea House, 1993. Learn more about the life of Pocahontas, from her friendship with the Jamestown colonists to her marriage to John Rolfe.

Schroeder, Alan. *Booker T. Washington, Educator.* New York: Chelsea House, 1992. Details the life of the former slave who grew up to found Tuskegee University, a college for black students.

Fiction

Denenberg, Barry. *When Will This Cruel War Be Over? The Civil War Diary of Emma Simpson, Gordonsville, Virginia, 1864.* New York: Scholastic, 1996. Emma Simpson of Gordonsville, Virginia, writes in her diary about the difficulties of growing up during the Civil War.

Henry, Marguerite. *Misty of Chincoteague.* New York: Simon and Schuster, 1988. A Newbery Honor book in 1948, this classic tells the story of Paul and Maureen, two children who want to own a wild pony from Chincoteague Island, Virginia. They try to buy and tame wild Phantom and her colt Misty.

Hermes, Patricia. *Our Strange New Land: Elizabeth's Diary, Jamestown, Virginia, 1609.* New York: Scholastic, 2000. Elizabeth and her family have just traveled from England to the New World. Settling in Jamestown, Virginia, Lizzie starts a journal describing the adventures in her new home.

Hermes, Patricia. *The Starving Time: Elizabeth's Diary, Book Two, Jamestown, Virginia, 1609.* New York: Scholastic, 2001. In the sequel to *Our Strange New Land*, Lizzie faces new problems as the colony struggles through a harsh winter with little food.

Pinkney, Andrea Davis. *Silent Thunder: A Civil War Story.* New York: Hyperion Books, 1999. Summer, a slave on a Virginia plantation in 1862, wants her brother to teach her to read—even though it's against the law. Her brother, however, has his own worries. He plans to find freedom through the help of the Underground Railroad.

WEBSITES

Commonwealth of Virginia
<http://www.state.va.us/>
Virginia's official website features information about living and working in Old Dominion, as well as links to history and geography sites.

Virginia Is for Lovers
<http://www.virginia.org>
This website includes a list of things to see and do in Virginia, and offers a list of historic sites, state parks, and events.

timesdispatch.com
<http://timesdispatch.com>
Get national, local, and feature stories at the online version of the *Richmond Times-Dispatch.*

Chesapeake Bay Program
<http://www.chesapeakebay.net/>
Find out more about the bay, from its marine life to cleanup efforts.

Welcome to Colonial Williamsburg
<http://www.history.org/>
Learn more about the restored former capital of Virginia, including a history of the site and visitor information.

A royal resident of Colonial Williamsburg goes for a carriage ride.

PRONUNCIATION GUIDE

Algonquian (al-GAHN-kwee-uhn)

Appalachian (ap-uh-LAY-chuhn)

Appomattox (ap-uh-MAT-uhks)

Assateague (AS-uh-TEEG)

Chesapeake (CHEHS-uh-PEEK)

Chincoteague (shing-kuh-TEEG)

Pocahontas (poh-kuh-HAHN-tuhs)

Powhatan (pow-uh-TAN)

Rappahannock (rap-uh-HAN-uhk)

Roanoke (ROH-uh-nohk)

Shenandoah (shehn-uhn-DOH-uh)

Susquehanna (suhs-kwuh-HAN-uh)

GLOSSARY

civil rights: the rights of all citizens—regardless of race, religion, sex—to enjoy life, liberty, property, and equal protection under the law

colony: a territory ruled by another country

constitution: the system of basic laws or rules of government, society, or organization; the document in which these laws or rules are written

immigrant: a person who moves into a foreign country and settles there

lagoon: a shallow lake or pond that joins a larger body of water

marsh: a spongy, treeless wetland soaked with water for long periods of time. Grasses are the main form of vegetation.

nutrient runoff: water from rain or melted snow that flows over land and carries nutrients from the ground to streams, lakes, oceans, and other bodies of water

peninsula: a stretch of land almost completely surrounded by water

plantation: a large estate, usually in a warm climate, where crops are grown by workers who live on the estate. In the past, plantation owners often used slave labor.

Reconstruction: the period from 1865 to 1877 during which the U.S. government brought the Southern states back into the Union after the Civil War. Before rejoining the Union, the Southern states had to pass laws allowing black men to vote. Places destroyed in the war were rebuilt and industries were developed.

swamp: a wetland permanently soaked with water. Trees and shrubs are the main form of vegetation.

INDEX

PHOTO ACKNOWLEDGMENTS

Cover photographs by © Jay Dickman/CORBIS (left), and © Joseph Sohm; ChromoSohm Inc./CORBIS (right). PresentationMaps.com, pp. 1, 8, 9, 51; © James L. Amos/CORBIS, pp. 2–3; © Buddy Mays/CORBIS, pp. 3, 4 (detail), 7 (detail), 17 (detail), 41 (detail), 55 (detail); © Pat and Chuck Blackley, pp. 6, 14, 61; Jeff Greenberg, pp. 7, 13, 15 (inset), 49; U.S. Fish and Wildlife Service, p. 10; Virginia Division of Tourism, pp. 11, 12, 15 (above), 24, 44 (both), 45, 48; The British Museum, pp. 16, 17; Virginia State Library and Archives, pp. 19, 21, 23, 27, 66 (bottom); U.S. Department of Interior, p. 20; © Bettmann/CORBIS, pp. 22, 36; National Park Service, Colonial National Historical Park, p. 25; Red Hill-The Patrick Henry National Memorial, Brookneal, Virginia, p. 26; Washington/Custis/Lee Collection, Washington and Lee University, Lexington, Virginia, p. 28; Architect of the Capitol, p. 29; © Collection of the New-York Historical Society, p. 31; Library of Congress, pp. 32, 67 (second from bottom), 69 (second from bottom); National Archives, p. 33; Birmingham Public Library, Birmingham, Alabama, p. 35; © Charles E. Rotkin/CORBIS, p. 37; © Michael Macor/San Francisco Chronicle/Corbis SABA, p. 39; Newport News Shipbuilding Co., pp. 40, 52; © Richard T. Nowitz/CORBIS, p. 42; Debra Ernst, Arlington County Government, p. 43; Lia Munst/Root Resources, p. 46; The Metro Chamber, p. 47; Virginia Coal Association, p. 50; Doyen Salsig, p. 54; Jerg Kroener, p. 55; © William J. Weber/Visuals Unlimited, p. 56; © M. Long/Visuals Unlimited, p. 57; © David Harp, p. 58; Jack Lindstrom, p. 60; Tim Seeley, pp. 63, 71 (top), 72; Photofest, p. 66 (top and second from bottom); David Merrick Productions, p. 66 (second from top); Montana Historical Society, pp. 67 (top), 68 (second from top); Hollywood Book & Poster Co., pp. 67 (second from top), 69 (top); Independent Picture Service, pp. 67 (bottom), 68 (top); Dale Olson & Associates, p. 68 (second from bottom); Houston Rockets, p. 68 (bottom); © CORBIS, p. 69 (second from top); Tom Victor, p. 69 (bottom); Jean Matheny, p. 70 (top); Laura Westlund, p. 70 (bottom); Michael Colopy, Chincoteague National Wildlife Refuge, p. 73; © W. Lynn Seldon Jr., p. 80.